# The Long Noon

## A Play

Patricia Chown

*Samuel French – London*
*New York – Sydney – Toronto – Hollywood*

---

### FOR AMATEUR PRODUCTION ENQUIRIES

#### UNITED  KINGDOM  AND  WORLD
#### EXCLUDING  NORTH  AMERICA
plays@SamuelFrench-London.co.uk
020 7255 4302/01

Each title is subject to availability from Samuel French,

depending upon country of performance.

---

# CHARACTERS

**Peter**
**Celia**
**Larry**
**Angela**
**Glenda**
**Sarah**
**Eileen**
**Voice**

The action takes place on the verandah of a large country house at noon on a hot summer's day

Time—the present

TO
MARIAN DAVISON

# THE LONG NOON*

*The verandah of a large country house. A hot summer's day. Noon*

*French windows at the back open into a large drawing-room. Beyond the verandah, out of sight, there are lawns and flower beds enclosed by a high wall with woods beyond. The drive to the road is off L. (It is suggested this play be performed with a curtain-setting containing openings where needed.) The verandah is furnished with chairs and stools for seven people. Jackets, cameras and other gear lie piled to one side*

*Music (e.g. Satie's piece for piano "Trois Gnossiennes") is heard for a few moments before the Lights come up to generate an atmosphere of mystery. Seven people are sitting around relaxed and apparently contented. They are Peter, a handsome man of fifty with a commanding presence; Celia, a sophisticated, elegant, attractive woman of forty; Larry, twenty-nine, rather ordinary-looking and unsure of himself; Angela, a rather sour woman of thirty-eight; Glenda, a plump, flabby sixty-six year old; Sarah, a heavily-built, slow-moving woman of forty-eight; Eileen, a quietly pretty but very diffident young woman of twenty-six. No-one speaks for a few seconds*

**Peter** Well, now we've introduced ourselves there seems to be nothing more to do at the moment.
**Sarah** (*stretching luxuriously*) Who cares on such a glorious day?
**Peter** I wonder when the others are coming.
**Sarah** What others?
**Peter** This can't be all—just seven of us.
**Glenda** Yes, I expected more.
**Celia** Funny there was only us in the coach.
**Eileen** I'm not worried. It's marvellous just to sit on this sunny verandah looking at the lawns and flowers and woods beyond.

---

It makes our miserable bit of grass at home look pathetic. I do so envy people who can afford to live in places like this. It isn't fair that other people should have so much.

**Angela** Why, where do you live, Eileen?

**Eileen** In a grotty suburb in South London.

**Angela** Poor you. I think it's lovely here too, but I'm beginning to wonder why no-one has appeared yet to greet us. We seem to have been waiting for ages. In fact I'm getting annoyed.

**Eileen** Perhaps whoever is in charge is coming down by car or in a later coach.

**Celia** That's probably the answer.

**Sarah** There *must* be staff around somewhere. Maybe they're all at the back preparing lunch. Lovely, the thought of being waited on.

**Glenda** I hope you're right. I expect someone will come and tell us when it's ready. I should think there will be seven courses at least.

**Angela** Huh! You're optimistic.

**Glenda** In the meantime I could do with a snack just to keep me going.

**Celia** I could do with a drink.

**Glenda** Me too. Something long and sweet and cold.

**Eileen** I wouldn't mind a cup of coffee. We must have spent at least two hours in the coach.

**Celia** I wasn't thinking of *that* kind of drink.

**Peter** (*getting up impatiently and moving downstage*) You women! Can't you think of anything but food and drink? Hasn't it struck any of you that there's something peculiar about this set-up? What's the time now? (*He looks at his watch*) Midday. We must have been sitting around here at least half an hour. The coach driver seemed to be positively moronic. As somebody said, there's been no-one to greet us or tell us what the day's programme is, and we can't even get into the house. Personally, I think it's a bloody insult.

**Celia** (*wearily*) He's off.

**Angela** I think he's right. I might have put it in stronger terms than that.

**Sarah** (*lazily*) What's all the fuss about? What's an insult? I'd be perfectly contented to sit here all day lazing in the sunshine as long as I get something to eat—don't much care what it is.

**Glenda** Hold on. I don't understand what you're talking about.
All I've come for is the food.
**Peter** (*contemptuously*) Food!
**Glenda** Yes. And I expect *haute cuisine* cooking.
**Angela** My invitation didn't say anything about food.
**Eileen** Nor mine.
**Peter** Of course they didn't. It was my impression that you'd come
to hear me give a talk on my plan for saving civilization. I've
thought more deeply about the subject than any man alive. I
know exactly what needs to be done. I've studied all the
religions, all the philosophies, all the sciences, and I've extracted
the kernel from each of them. They're mostly false of course.
That's why civilization has gone so wrong. But my plan can save
the world.

*Sarah stifles a yawn*

**Celia** (*sarcastically*) Bravo!
**Eileen** (*admiringly*) Fancy being able to talk about those things. I
wish *I* could.
**Angela** Not exactly modest, are you?
**Peter** I don't believe in false modesty.
**Celia** As I well know.
**Eileen** Have you two met before?
**Celia** Unfortunately.
**Peter** A *very* long time ago.
**Eileen** Sorry, I shouldn't have asked.
**Celia** Actually Peter and I were once married.
**Peter** You didn't have to drag that up. That belongs to the past.
**Celia** A very dead past.
**Angela** For heaven's sake don't start wrangling. I came here to get
away from all that. Everywhere I go people start to quarrel.
**Peter** But you did all come to hear my lecture?
**Celia** Not me for one. I know it practically by heart already.
**Sarah** I certainly didn't come here to be lectured.
**Glenda** Nor me.
**Peter** There must be some misunderstanding. Did everyone get an
invitation?
**Eileen** Yes.
**Glenda** Yes.

*The others indicate "Yes"*

**Angela** You've told us why you're here. But where was your invitation from? What did it say?

**Peter** (*taking a letter from his pocket and reading*) "Dear Professor Wilton."

**Eileen** (*impressed*) Professor!

**Peter** (*continuing reading*) "We shall be honoured if you will address this organization on the subject of the achievement of world peace about which we know you have wide knowledge. Subject to your confirmation you will be driven to the Conference Centre by coach as there are no facilities for parking. The pick-up point is in Grosvenor Street at ten a.m. on Sunday September Fourth. We shall be most disappointed if you are unable to come. Yours" etc.

**Angela** *My* invitation didn't say anything like that.

**Eileen** Nor mine.

**Angela** Where was it from?

**Peter** The Society for the Establishment of World Peace. I must admit I hadn't heard of its existence.

**Angela** Nor me. What's the address?

**Peter** One hundred and three St James Terrace. It's obviously a hoax. I've been made a fool of and I don't like it.

**Angela** I don't think you're the only one. I'm getting more furious every moment. I thought I came here to escape from irritations and certainly not to be lectured. Actually I've been seething ever since that fool of a driver ordered me to sit at the back of the coach when it wasn't even a quarter full.

**Eileen** Why did you stay put?

**Angela** (*hesitantly*) I—I didn't want to give him the satisfaction.

**Sarah** Well stop seething and enjoy the day.

**Peter** If you can enjoy yourself when you've been made a fool of then *I* can't.

**Glenda** Why don't we all tell what we were invited *for*, instead of getting scratchy? My invitation was sent from the same address but was to enjoy a day of *haute cuisine* cooking. As there's nothing I enjoy better than good nosh, I naturally accepted by return.

**Peter** What about you, Celia?

**Celia** My invitation was to see a rare collection of jewels and carved jade. I love beautiful things.

**Peter** (*dryly*) As I remember. (*After a pause*) Sarah?

**Sarah** A day when I should be waited on hand and foot. No need
to lift a finger.

**Glenda** It doesn't look to me as though anybody's likely to be
waited on hand and foot. And as for the *haute cuisine*, it's my
guess we shall be lucky if we get bread and cheese. (*Sighing*) I've
a beautiful little chicken at home and asparagus and a bottle of
wine all sitting in the fridge. (*After a pause*) You're right,
Professor, it's a hoax.

**Angela** One great bloody hoax.

**Peter** Wait a moment. What about you, Eileen?

**Eileen** I was invited to enjoy the kind of surroundings I've always
hankered after; to experience a life style I've only dreamed of.

**Celia** What have you dreamed of?

**Eileen** Wonderful surroundings—like this—a lovely home, gor-
geous clothes. But more than that, to be beautiful and elegant
and clever and admired by everybody.

**Angela** (*scathingly*) You didn't expect *all* that, did you?

**Eileen** Of course not. But why is it some people have everything? I
do so envy them. (*To Celia*) You're elegant and beautiful and
probably clever. I'm not even clever.

**Celia** Cleverness on its own won't get you far, my dear.

**Eileen** I wouldn't know about that.

**Peter** (*a bit impatiently*) One thing is obvious. We've all been
brought here under false pretences.

**Celia** Hang on a moment, we haven't heard from Larry.

**Larry** (*embarrassed*) I'd rather not say. Sorry.

**Angela** (*a bit spitefully*) Wasn't a blue film show or something like
that?

**Larry** Of course not.

**Eileen** What an unkind thing to say.

**Angela** It made him blush.

**Larry** Oh stow it.

**Angela** (*mockingly*) Temper.

**Eileen** Leave him alone.

*Larry gives Eileen a grateful look and she smiles at him*

**Peter** As I said, we've all been brought here under false pretences.
But why? Why? And what are we going to do about it?

**Angela** I know what I could have done.

**Celia** What was that?

**Angela** Taken part in an anti-racist demo.

**Sarah** That would hardly have been a rest from irritation.

**Angela** That's why I chose this instead. In fact I'm getting more bloody angry every moment. I'm not naturally bad tempered — only when there's a good reason.

**Glenda** We don't even know when the coach is coming to fetch us.

**Angela** *If* it is.

**Eileen** (*afraid*) Don't say that.

**Glenda** What I *do* know is that I'm starving. I'd go and find out what's happening in the kitchen if we could get into the house. I'm going to try that window again.

**Celia** But you know it was locked when I tried it earlier.

*Glenda goes upstage to the french window and it opens easily*

**Glenda** How strange. It opens.

**Celia** I swear it was locked before.

*Glenda pushes the french window open and takes one step into the room*

**Glenda** Good Lord! We may not have been hoaxed after all. Come and look, Celia.

*Celia goes to the french window and looks inside*

**Celia** (*wonderingly*) It's an exhibition of jewellery and jade like they said. I must have a proper look. Anyone else coming?

**Glenda** You can't eat jewels. But I'm going to see if I can get through to the domestic quarters.

*Glenda joins Celia and they both disappear into the house*

**Eileen** I'm not going inside that place for anything. There's something funny about it. First the door is locked, then it isn't.

**Peter** Celia probably didn't try hard enough the first time.

**Eileen** I still don't like it, it gives me the shivers.

**Larry** I think you're letting your imagination run away with you. Let's go and explore the grounds. I could do with a stretch.

**Eileen** All right, it's better than just hanging around waiting for something to happen.

**Angela** My guess is that bloody nothing is going to happen.

**Larry** (*getting up and holding out his hand to Eileen*) Come on then.

*Eileen and Larry go off together* R

**Angela**  I've got a strong suspicion that whatever Glenda finds, it isn't going to be food, and I'm getting hungry. Did either of you notice a village or shops before the coach turned into the avenue?

**Peter**  Can't say I did.

**Angela**  Well I'm going to wander down to the road to find out. Coming, Sarah? We might at least find a pub or a shop where we can get some chocolate or biscuits.

**Sarah**  Isn't it a bit far?

**Angela**  The gates can't be more than seven minutes walk away.

**Sarah**  I don't think I've got the energy.

**Angela**  Yes, you have.

**Sarah**  Oh, all right. You'll have to help me out of this chair.

*Angela does so*

Oh dear, I'm quite stiff.

**Angela**  Got your handbag?

**Sarah**  Oh no, I almost forgot.

*Sarah takes her handbag from the pile in the corner, then joins Angela and they go off together L*

*Peter is left alone on the verandah. He looks at his watch and sees that it has stopped. He shakes it, listens to it, then gives up. He fetches his portfolio and takes out the script of the speech he was to have given. He starts to read it aloud then continues without looking at it*

**Peter**  "Mr President, Ladies and Gentlemen, I know that you have come here today to hear me talk on a subject very close to all our hearts. This is our growing anxiety about the degenerating state of the world today. The wars, the famines, the crimes, the brutalities, the corruption, the sense of hopelessness because ordinary people like you and I feel we can do nothing to halt it."

*Celia appears at the french window and stands listening, but unimpressed. She is clasping a small object tightly in her hand*

"But it is *not* hopeless and I know the solution. I promise you that if you trust and act on my advice, I can lead you out of the morass. Everything has a beginning and every journey has a first step." (*He pauses*)

**Celia** (*ironically*) Bravo. Would you like me to carry on from there for you? After all I know that speech word for word.
**Peter** No you don't damn you. I've rewritten a lot of it since your time.
**Celia** Not that much I'll be bound. It amazes me that you're still getting away with it. I rather thought you'd given up—or gone to the United States where people are more easily gulled.
**Peter** You always have tried to make me feel less than I am. You never believed in me.
**Celia** I did at the beginning—until I discovered that behind your conceit is nothing but a straw man. You can't impress me—not any longer. (*She moves downstage to pick up her handbag and quickly slips the object she is holding into it and takes out a handkerchief*)
**Peter** What did you put into your handbag?
**Celia** Nothing. I just wanted a tissue.

*Peter goes to Celia swiftly, and snatches the bag from her*

Hey! Of all the bloody nerve. What do you think——?

*He fishes about in the bag and produces a jade ornament*

**Peter** (*holding it out*) So you're still up to your tricks.
**Celia** No, no I'm not, it belongs to me.
**Peter** Don't give me that. Anyway I can soon find out.

*Peter goes in to the room*

*Celia sinks on to a chair feeling deflated. She covers her face with her hands*

*Peter returns*

Jade Buddha circa eighth century. I was able to put it back in its place because the label was there. That room is a treasure house. I should have thought you would have learned to keep your hands off what doesn't belong to you by this time. Some people never learn.
**Celia** It's only that I find it difficult to resist beautiful things.
**Peter** Even when they don't belong to you. That's a very pretty necklace you're wearing. Did you pinch that?
**Celia** It was given to me. And please don't talk so loudly someone might hear you.

**Peter** (*looking around*) There isn't a soul in sight.
**Celia** You may not believe this, but that was the first thing I've taken since—since the—er—case.
**Peter** The correct word is stolen.
**Celia** How cruel you are.
**Peter** I suppose you were going to say it's the first thing you've stolen since the Police caught up with you.
**Celia** Yes, it's true, I swear it.
**Peter** That court case. I shall never forget it—having to get up in the witness box and commit perjury for your sake.
**Celia** You didn't have to. You could have spoken the truth.
**Peter** What! Admit to the world that my wife was a habitual thief? I don't know how you got away with it all those years. It didn't lessen the humiliation though. I don't know which was harder to bear—the pity or the sneers.
**Celia** And how do you think *I* felt?
**Peter** You? I reckon you got off lightly. You could have been sent to jail instead of referred for psychiatric treatment.
**Celia** And deprived of my home.
**Peter** No need to put it like that. I bought you a flat and let you have the choice of the furniture. After all, our marriage was already on the rocks. That court case and the meal the press made of it was the last straw. That's what was most humiliating.
**Celia** To your self-image, your pride.
**Peter** (*shrugging*) Put it like that if it gives you any satisfaction.

*Pause*

**Celia** Shall I tell you what the psychiatrist made me realize?
**Peter** If you like.
**Celia** That it was you who turned me into a kleptomaniac.
**Peter** (*after an astonished pause*) Me! I never heard such nonsense in my life.
**Celia** How is it then that I never took a single thing that wasn't mine until after our marriage although I've loved beautiful objects all my life? Of course I often wanted to possess them but I didn't *steal*. And after we parted I didn't take anything until you turned up today.
**Peter** I refuse to take the blame for your aberrations.
**Celia** The psychiatrist said I stole because I was starved of love. He said sub-consciously I was trying to compensate.

**Peter**  Compensate for what?

**Celia**  Your love.

**Peter**  I did love you in the beginning.

**Celia**  Because I was beautiful and you liked being seen with me. Later you got bored and irritated because I couldn't keep up intellectually with your grand friends.

**Peter**  And then you began to undermine me. Me! To make me feel that you despised me. *You* of all people.

**Celia**  That was later when I realized you were a phoney, an intellectual con man. When I'd heard you say the same things over and over again like an old gramophone record and I couldn't be proud of you—or admire you any more. I suppose I was a fool to be taken in by you. But it wasn't just that that made me stop loving you. It was the terrible hurtful things you said—anything to humiliate me. (*She breaks down and sobs*)

*Peter watches helplessly then goes to her*

**Peter**  Please, please don't cry like that.

**Celia**  Oh God. I wish I'd never come here today. And why the two of us after so many years and for quite different reasons?

**Peter**  (*thoughtfully*)  Like the others. All for different reasons.

*Celia powders her nose and puts on her lipstick*

Better?

*Celia just nods*

I thought at first someone was just playing a practical joke on us, though a damned unfunny one, but now . . .

**Celia**  It isn't a joke at all is it?

**Peter**  No. God knows what it is.

*Pause*

**Celia**  Peter.

**Peter**  Mmm?

**Celia**  I'm sorry I was so bitchy to you earlier.

**Peter**  Forget it.

**Eileen**  (*off*)  No! No! Let me go! Let me go!

*Eileen runs in from R looking distraught*

**Celia**  (*standing*)  What on earth has happened?

**Eileen** That ghastly Larry. He—he—I was frightened.

**Celia** Do you mean he got tough?

**Eileen** He must be crazy. I let him kiss me and then he sort of lost control. It was horrible. He seemed like a wild animal. He—it was awful!

**Celia** (*leading Eileen to a chair*) Come and sit down. Poor child, you're shaking.

**Eileen** No-one's ever behaved like that to me before.

**Peter** I wish there was something we could give her.

**Celia** She needs a drink.

**Peter** No hope of that I'm afraid in this benighted place. I wonder if Angela and Sarah have had any luck. They seem to have been away a long time.

**Celia** And so has Glenda. Perhaps she's had some luck in the kitchen quarters.

**Peter** I doubt it.

**Eileen** (*looking off* R *and seeing Larry*) He's coming back. (*She gets up*) I can't face him. Where can I go?

**Celia** Why not go to meet the others? They went down the avenue.

**Eileen** I'll do that. Sorry I made such a fool of myself.

*Eileen hurries off* L

**Peter** Phew! It's turned sultry. Feels like a storm gathering.

**Celia** If at this moment you asked me to choose between the finest jewel in the world and a glass of spring water. I'd opt for the water.

**Peter** Me too.

*Pause—they look at one another with kindness*

**Celia** Peter . . .

**Peter** Yes?

**Celia** I'm glad you found out about—about the jade carving. I don't feel I shall ever be tempted to do it again. I'm sort of free. Thank you.

**Peter** I'm the last person in the world to thank. I'm sorry I was such a brute.

**Celia** That's the first time I've ever heard you say you were sorry. You've always been so proud.

**Peter** (*hesitantly*) Celia.

**Celia** Yes?

**Peter** I don't know how . . .

*Larry enters from* R, *looking troubled*

**Larry** Where is she? Eileen I mean . . .
**Celia** I think she went to look for Sarah and Angela.
**Larry** I suppose she told you about . . . (*He stops, too embarassed to continue*) I must go after her to apologize.
**Celia** I shouldn't—not just now. You did give her rather a fright.
**Larry** Something seemed to take possession of me. She did sort of lead me on.
**Celia** She's a bit of an innocent I think. (*After a pause*) You like girls, don't you?
**Larry** Like? That's putting it mildly. They torment me. Sometimes I think I'll go crazy. You see they never seem to fancy me. My life is one long brush off. (*To Peter*) I bet yours hasn't been.
**Peter** You'd be surprised.
**Larry** It hurts so. I feel like—like a nothing.
**Peter** We all have to grow our own armour.
**Larry** How? When? Shall I always make a mess of things?
**Celia** Of course you won't. But there is a time and a place.
**Larry** I thought that's what today would be.
**Peter** You mean you expected to meet girls here? That this would be a kind of whore-house?

*Larry nods miserably*

(*Bursting into laughter*) Oh you poor misguided loon. I'm beginning to see the funny side of this.
**Larry** (*fiercely*) Don't laugh at me!
**Peter** Sorry, Larry, I'm not laughing at you but at the lot of us. I suppose I ought to be angry. I can't normally stomach being made a fool of but somehow this is all too ridiculous. Celia here is the only one to get what she came for, but not in the way she expected. Who in God's name is behind it?
**Celia** Or what?
**Peter** Exactly. (*After a pause*) What do you make the time, Larry?
**Larry** (*looking at his watch*) That's funny—twelve o'clock. It must be more than that. (*He listens to his watch*) It's stopped.
**Peter** So did mine at twelve o'clock.
**Celia** (*getting up and moving downstage*) I don't like it. I'm frightened.

**Peter** (*going to her and putting an arm round her*) Calm down, darling. There must be a logical explanation. A sunspot or something.

**Celia** That doesn't explain the invitations.

*Glenda enters through the french windows*

**Glenda** There's something damn funny about this place—at least about the house.

**Larry** How do you mean?

**Glenda** It's as bare as a picked bone, except that one room just through there. That looks like a damned jewellers shop.

**Larry** What!

**Peter** You don't mean the house is empty?

**Glenda** Yes.

**Celia** (*thoughtfully*) I don't think I'm in the least surprised.

**Glenda** The kitchen is enormous. A great sink, old rusty range, butler's pantry, larder. But not a bite of food. It was after seeing the kitchen that I decided to have a look at the rest of the house. As I went into one empty room after the other, all as silent as tombs, no sound except my own footsteps and my own breathing, I got the heebie-jeebies, I can tell you. I'm damned glad to be out here with other human beings.

*Eileen returns, looking scared*

**Celia** Eileen! What's the matter? Where are the others?

**Eileen** I changed my mind and left the drive. There was an—an apple orchard.

**Glenda** (*eagerly*) With apples?

**Eileen** It was horrible. There were apples—hundreds of them. I went to pick one and it was rotten. They all are. Like in a nightmare. (*She covers her face with her hands*)

**Glenda** What sort of damned place is this?

**Peter** Perhaps it *is* damned. A hell where no time passes.

**Eileen** (*a bit hysterical*) Don't talk like that!

*Larry goes to Eileen and puts an arm over her shoulders protectively. She tries to move away*

**Larry** Eileen—please.

*She looks at him and is reassured*

Come and sit down.

*Eileen allows Larry to lead her to a chair. He sits beside her*

*A moment later Angela appears from* L *with Sarah puffing along behind her*

**Glenda** I am glad to see *you.* Did you have any luck with food?
**Sarah** We're p-prisoners.
**Peter** What do you mean?
**Sarah** The gates have disappeared.
**Eileen** I don't understand. The gates where we came in?
**Angela** There's nothing there but a continuation of that seven foot high wall that surrounds this ruddy place.
**Peter** That's impossible.
**Angela** It's true I tell you.
**Glenda** Perhaps you wandered away from the avenue.
**Angela** How could we? It's a gravelled drive. There are no paths to wander on to. We're not a couple of fools.
**Sarah** That's right. (*She sinks into a chair*)
**Angela** (*angrily*) It's outrageous. When I get out of this place I'm going to create such a stink that——
**Celia** (*breaking in*) *If* we get out.
**Eileen** Please don't talk like that it frightens me. (*She gives Larry an appealing look*)
**Larry** Of course we shall.
**Angela** Can you suggest how? We *saw* the wall.
**Celia** (*quietly*) Has anyone noticed that the sun hasn't moved since we arrived. It's still almost directly overhead. It's still noon.
**Peter** Good God! That's why our watches have stopped.
**Larry** You're saying that—I don't believe it! I don't believe it! Time *can't* stop.
**Peter** (*quietly*) It seems that it has.

*Everyone falls silent with horror*

**Eileen** I wish I hadn't come. (*She whimpers*)
**Peter** Let's try to be sensible. Let's try to consider our predicament logically.
**Angela** Logical be damned! Here we are trapped in this weird dump where nothing makes sense. What's logical about that?

**Glenda**  We were lured here.
**Sarah**  And all for different reasons.
**Peter**  So let's try to examine the reasons calmly.
**Angela**  I feel too furious to examine *anything* calmly.
**Larry**  So where do we begin?

*Angela and Glenda sit*

**Peter**  At the beginning. (*After a pause*) The invitations, our
  reasons for accepting. Then——
**Angela**  And where does that get us?
**Peter**  I don't know. But at least let's try it. It's essential to be
  honest with ourselves and with one another.
**Angela**  I don't hold with truth games.
**Celia**  This isn't a game.
**Peter**  (*after looking round*) We'll begin with you, Eileen.
**Eileen**  Why me?
**Peter**  I've a feeling you've the least to hide.
**Eileen**  All right, if it will help. (*After a pause*) As I told you, I was
  invited to experience a new life style—luxury, and all that. It's
  something I've always envied. I've never had anything I wanted.
  Looks or lovely clothes or brains. I've never been good at
  anything. I did so envy the clever or popular girls at school. I've
  never even had a boy-friend. There was once a man at the office,
  but when the pretty new typist came—well, that was that.
**Larry**  (*sincerely*) I find that hard to believe. I think you're pretty.
**Eileen**  You're just saying that.
**Larry**  No—really.

*Eileen gives Larry a grateful smile*

**Peter**  (*to Larry*) You told Celia and me. But for the sake of the
  others let's put it into a nutshell. You thought you were going to
  meet a collection of—er—how shall I put it?
**Angela**  We can guess.
**Larry**  (*ashamed*) As I've explained to Celia and Peter, girls don't
  usually go for me and sometimes it's worse than humiliating.
  (*To Eileen*) Look at the way you reacted when I made a pass at
  you. Though I thought it was what you wanted
**Eileen**  I think I half did really. I'm sorry.
**Angela**  (*nastily*) Well, well, what other revelations are we going to
  get?

**Peter** (*pointedly ignoring her*) It's plain, Glenda, that you came for the food.

**Glenda** (*indignantly*) What's wrong with that? True I do adore good food but I see no harm in it. Anyway no-one could say I was actually greedy.

**Angela** Huh!

**Peter** I'm not too clear about you, Angela.

**Angela** It's simple enough. I merely wanted a bit of freedom from aggro. It happens all the time at home and at work. Sometimes I get so angry I could commit murder. As for today it's been the most maddening and frustrating of my life. In fact if I could lay my hands on whoever is responsible I'd ... (*Words fail her*)

**Peter** OK, OK. (*To Sarah*) You say you came for a rest.

**Sarah** Yes and I'd have had it if there hadn't been so much arguing and bellyaching—especially from Angela.

**Angela** Of all the nerve!

**Peter** Cool it, everybody. What we're trying to find out is why we're here.

**Angela** What *I'd* like to know is how and when we're going to get away.

**Peter** (*to Celia*) We all know you came to see an exhibition of jewellery and jade.

**Glenda** Strange you were the only one who got what you were promised.

**Celia** To tempt me. Perhaps that was the point.

**Angela** What are you talking about?

**Celia** I'll tell you——

**Peter** There's no need, Celia.

**Celia** They've a right to know. (*After a slight pause*) I love to possess beautiful things so much I couldn't resist stealing one of them.

**Angela** (*startled*) *You?* Steal?

**Eileen** But you seem to have so much already. I can't understand why a person like you should need to do that.

**Angela** So what did you do with this object you pinched?

**Celia** Peter put it back. You see he knows me.

**Peter** So that only leaves me. I was invited to lecture to a non-existent audience. It just doesn't make sense.

**Celia** Would it have changed anything if you'd given your talk?

**Peter** I thought so. I was so sure I and only I knew all the answers.

Now I'm not sure that I know anything. (*After a pause*) I feel—
hollow.
**Angela**  So where does that get us?
**Peter**  Wait.

*Peter looks thoughtfully at eveyone in turn. Glenda, Angela and*
*Sarah shift uncomfortably under his gaze*

My God! I've got it.
**Larry**  What?
**Peter**  The seven deadly sins.

*The Lights dim slightly*

**Angela**  What the hell are you talking about?
**Glenda**  I can't even remember what they are. No—wait a minute
the only one I can think of is gluttony, and that certainly doesn't
apply to *me*.
**Peter**  I'm not accusing anybody. I think I've learned what mine is
**Celia**  Me too.
**Angela**  I think you're talking a lot of shit. We're no nearer
discovering why we were brought to this Godforsaken dump
place and, more important, how we're going to get out of it
Christ Almighty! If I——

*The Lights dim even more and there is a roll of thunder*

**Eileen** (*startled, putting her hands over her ears*)  Oh!

*Another roll of thunder*

**Glenda** (*sarcastically*)  Careful, Angela. You don't want to offend
the Almighty.
**Eileen**  I'm afraid of thunder.

*The Lights become very bright. A voice of great authority is heard*

**Voice**  You have nothing to fear, my child.
**Eileen** (*looking about her*)  Who are you? Where are you?
**Voice**  That isn't important. Just listen.
**Eileen**  Yes, yes, I'm listening.
**Glenda**  What's the matter with *her*. I can't hear anything.
**Angela**  Nor me.
**Peter** (*who has also heard the Voice*)  Sssh.
**Angela** (*indignantly*)  Don't you sssh me!

*Celia and Larry have also heard the Voice. They, together with Eileen and Peter, get to their feet*

**Voice** I have brought you here to give you the opportunity to see yourselves as you are before it is too late. Some of you are blind and may never see. But there are those among you who have seen. So remember what you have been shown.
**Celia** (*fervently*) Oh, I will.
**Larry** And I.
**Voice** It is easy to forget. But you have the possibility of making new beginnings—always and at any moment—if only you remember.
**Angela** Just look at them. I reckon they've lost their marbles.
**Sarah** (*wistfully*) Then I wish I had too.
**Voice** My dear children—Celia, Eileen, Larry, Peter—blessings and goodbye.

*A distant peal of thunder*

(*Fainter*) Goodbye.
**Eileen** (*full of wonder*) He knows our names.

*Pause*

**Celia** The voice was so beautiful. No—more than beautiful.
**Angela** There wasn't any voice. You're crazy.

*There is the sound of the coach in the distance*

**Sarah** Wait, I can hear something now. But it's for real. A car engine. (*She points off* L) Look, it's the coach just turning into the drive. (*After a pause*) Now it's stopped.
**Glenda** But you said there was a wall.
**Angela** Does that matter? It was obviously some kind of trick. We've been a victim of trickery. The point is, the coach is back. I can't get to it fast enough.

**Sarah**
**Glenda** } (*together*) Nor me.

*Sarah, Angela and Glenda hurriedly collect their belongings and leave*

*Larry gathers up his own and Eileen's things*

**Larry** (*to Celia*) Before I go—thank you for being so understanding.

**Celia** It was nothing.
**Eileen** You helped me too. You were ever so kind.

*Celia goes to Eileen and kisses her*

**Celia** Good luck, my dear, and be happy.
**Larry** (*taking Eileen by the hand*) Time to go.

   *Larry and Eileen leave*

*Celia wanders over to pick up her coat*

**Peter** Celia . . .
**Celia** Yes?
**Peter** It is't going to be goodbye is it? Perhaps even——
**Celia** (*breaking in*) I don't know, Peter. Don't say any more just
   now. It's all been so strange.
**Peter** Just as you say. I can wait.
**Celia** Thank you. (*She goes to him and kisses him lightly*)

*The hooting of the coach horn is heard*

   *Peter picks up his jacket and briefcase and they both leave*

*The music is heard again for a few moments*

CURTAIN

# FURNITURE AND PROPERTY LIST

*On stage:* Chairs and stools for seven
Cameras
**Eileen**'s cardigan
**Peter**'s jacket and portfolio containing speech
**Celia**'s coat and handbag containing handkerchief, lipstick and
face power
**Sarah**'s handbag
**Glenda**'s handbag
**Angela**'s handbag

*Off stage:* Small jade object **(Celia)**

*Personal:* **Peter:** letter in pocket, wristwatch
**Celia:** necklace
**Larry:** wristwatch

# LIGHTING PLOT

Property fittings required: nil

Exterior. The same scene throughout

*To open:* Blackout

| | | |
|---|---|---|
| *Cue* 1 | When music fades<br>*Bring up lighting* | (Page 1) |
| *Cue* 2 | **Peter**: "The seven deadly sins."<br>*Dim lighting slightly* | (Page 17) |
| *Cue* 3 | **Angela**: "Christ Almighty! If I ——"<br>*Dim lighting further* | (Page 17) |
| *Cue* 4 | **Eileen**: "I'm afraid of thunder."<br>*Bring up very bright lighting* | (Page 17) |

# EFFECTS PLOT

| | | |
|---|---|---|
| *Cue* 1 | To open<br>*Music* | (Page 1) |
| *Cue* 2 | **Angela**: "Christ Almighty!" If I ——" <br>*Roll of thunder* | (Page 17) |
| *Cue* 3 | **Eileen**: "Oh!" <br>*Roll of thunder* | (Page 17) |
| *Cue* 4 | **Voice**: "— blessings and goodbye" <br>*Distant peal of thunder* | (Page 18) |
| *Cue* 5 | **Angela**: "You're crazy." <br>*Sound of coach engine approaching in the distance and drawing up* | (Page 18) |
| *Cue* 6 | **Celia** goes to **Peter** and kisses him lightly <br>*Coach horn hooting* | (Page 19) |
| *Cue* 7 | **Peter** and **Celia** leave <br>*Music* | (Page 19) |

9 780573 121432